# NATIONAL LAMPOON®
## TOTALLY
# TRUE FACTS

# NATIONAL LAMPOON®

## *TOTALLY*

## TRUE FACTS

A Brand-New Collection of Absurd-but-True
Real-Life Funny Stuff

COMPILED BY JASON WARD

**CB**

CONTEMPORARY
BOOKS

CHICAGO

To the swarm of True Facts contributors
who have remained loyal
throughout the past twenty-five years.
Even after we abolished
our free T-shirt policy.

## ACKNOWLEDGMENTS

Special thanks to Jim Jimirro, David Garrett, Linda Gray, Willie Harper, and John Bendel.

1

# MISSING DOG HEAD

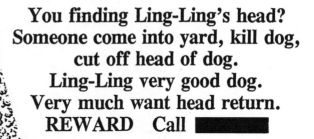

You finding Ling-Ling's head?
Someone come into yard, kill dog,
cut off head of dog.
Ling-Ling very good dog.
Very much want head return.
REWARD   Call ▬▬▬▬

It's 6 a.m.
Do you know
where
Grandpa is?

Ad contributed by Dana Willey

# Commissioner Davis To Head "Assault On Literacy Month"

From the *Pahokee (Florida) Sun*; contributed by Donald Vaughan

# Sadness Is No. 1 Reason Men and Women Cry

From the *Omaha World Herald*; contributed by Josh Hamilton

# April slated as child abuse month

# Get in the car, kids, Daddy has a surprise!

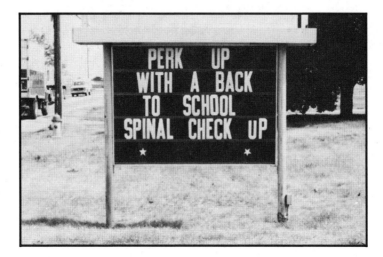

Photo contributed by Sherrie Roden

# Our mistake

Liberal MP Sheila Copps did not direct cries of "scumbag" at the Government benches in the House of Commons as reported yesterday. As recorded by Hansard, her comments were, "Who is a scumbag?" followed by, "The honorable member just called us a scumbag."

A Nov. 9 Southam News story about Nova Scotia's black minority was accompanied by an inaccurate photograph caption. The photo, said to depict rundown homes outside Dartmouth, was actually of a pig farm. *The Citizen* apologises for the error.

# Correction

The mock penile implant procedure pictured on Monday's Close-Up page was photographed at Mercy Hospital, not, as the cutline read, at Baystate Medical Center.

Ha! And to think they all laughed at me in hand modeling school!

— Wanted —
# HAND MODEL
## WITH MISSING FINGERS
Television movie production needs female hand model with 3 missing fingers.

**Call Steve at**

**Hi, I'm interested in buying a house . . . *OUCH!***

Photo contributed by Bill Stuehler

**So show some respect, you.**

Photo contributed by David D. Jarvis

Photo contributed by Wendy Cowdon

Mom, how did you and Dad meet?

I'M the guy that stroked your thigh at the Penn game. Please identify yourself (what you had on, seat number, etc.) so I know it's you. ███

PERSON WHO'S putting clawmarks on my husband's back, would you please doctor him or lay off one. Otherwise, be fore-warned of the consequences. W.N.

## PERSONAL

WANTED: Female who can reproduce asexually. Call Stan at 11-2 ███

From the *Louisville* (Kentucky) *News-Enterprise*; contributed by Neil and Nancy Langford

We want to give you something to make your child vomit.

It's called Syrup of Ipecac. And every house should have some.

It's powerful medicine. A tablespoon will make your child vomit in less than 15 minutes. Not a pretty thought. But it's a lifesaver to the child who has accidentally swallowed poison.

This year, an estimated 500,000 children will be victims of accidental poisoning. Unfortunately, some of them will die.

Too many times this tragedy could be avoided if only there was Syrup of Ipecac in the medicine cabinet. Syrup of Ipecac can get the poison out – fast.

That's why Community Hospital wants to give you a free bottle. If you have a child under the age of 5, simply send in the coupon below. We'll send you a 1 oz. bottle of Syrup of Ipecac along with a brochure on what to do if your child or anyone in your family swallows poison.

At Community Hospital, we're always here when you need us. But, frankly, we want to do everything we can to see you never do.

Name

Street

City_____ State_____ Zip___

COMMUNITY HOSPITAL OF ROANOKE VALLEY
*Caring for Your Life and Lifestyle*

**National Poison Prevention Week**
**March 18-24**

15

Photo contributed by Jay Goldstein

Photo contributed by F. H. Martin

Photo contributed by Liz Lindsey

**So, what was it like? Was Mary cute? What was Moses wearing?**

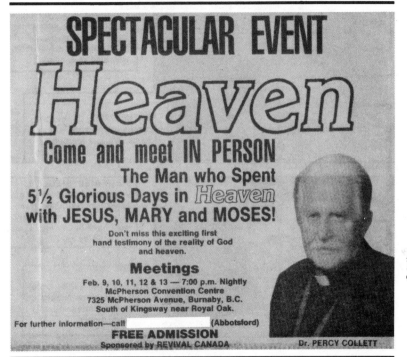

Ad from the (Vancouver, British Columbia) *Province*; contributed by Pat Bell

# Specialized law.

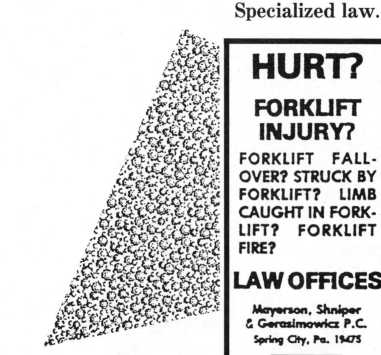

**HURT?**

**FORKLIFT INJURY?**

FORKLIFT FALL-OVER? STRUCK BY FORKLIFT? LIMB CAUGHT IN FORK-LIFT? FORKLIFT FIRE?

**LAW OFFICES**

Mayerson, Shniper & Gerasimowicz P.C.
Spring City, Pa. 19475

# Confucius says . . .

Photo contributed by Chris Van Hasselt

The Shadow At Bay

Jackson Cole

WALT SLADE

Kr. 3.25

Hingsten strakk ut så den formerlig fløy over bakken i det ville kappløpet med døden...

Fart, Shadow, Fart!

Photo contributed by Mark Mattison

CLASSIC MOVIE

Scarlet Street

Tonight, Edward G. Robinson falls for a prostitute and pays for it.

Arts & Entertainment Network

Surprise Your Eyes!

June 22nd at 8:00 pm

From Manhattan Cable TV's *Cable Guide*; contributed by Frank Mastropolo

# I don't care how you stir up business, just do it!

Photo contributed by Luke Softich

# Emergencies only.

Photo contributed by Nuhki Ciammi

# Carbon man sets himself on fire

From the (Allentown, Pennsylvania) *Morning Call*; contributed by H. D. Klopp

## Bad diapers draw crowd

## Fire damage heavy to Torch Oil Co.

## Iran Claims Success In Its Attacks On Iran

# Women protest charge of causing drought

**NIAMEY, Niger** — Hundreds of women marched yesterday to protest being harassed by people who blame them for a shortage of rainfall in this impoverished nation on the fringes of the Sahara Desert.

The march was organized by the Niger Women's Association and the Niger Human Rights Association after some young women wearing short skirts were blamed for the drought and stripped in public.

Men who falsely claim to be Muslim holy men, known here as marabouts, have asserted that the women's dress was responsible for the lower-than-normal rainfall this year.

Police also interrogated women whose clothes were deemed indecent.

# Look, honey, they're having a sale today!

Photo contributed by Larry Koepsell

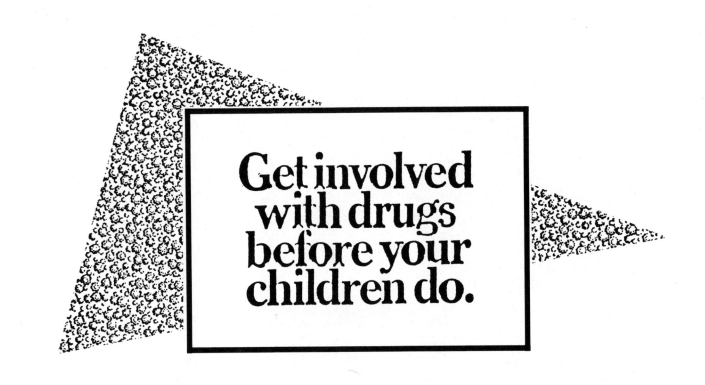

Get involved with drugs before your children do.

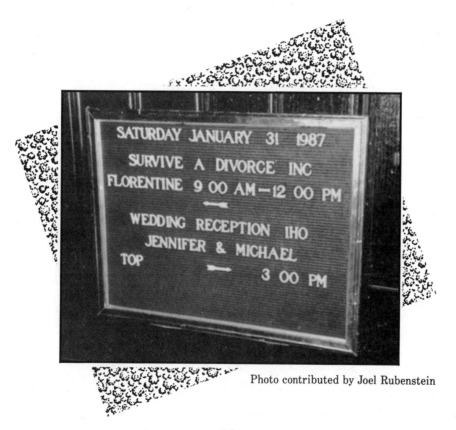

SATURDAY JANUARY 31 1987

SURVIVE A DIVORCE INC
FLORENTINE 9 00 AM—12 00 PM
—
WEDDING RECEPTION IHO
JENNIFER & MICHAEL
TOP
—        3 00 PM

Photo contributed by Joel Rubenstein

I agree with his politics, but he seems to have an inferiority complex.

Photo contributed
by Michael Nigro

**"Hey honey, what did you say your nickname was back in college?"**

Photo contributed by Bobbie Scannell

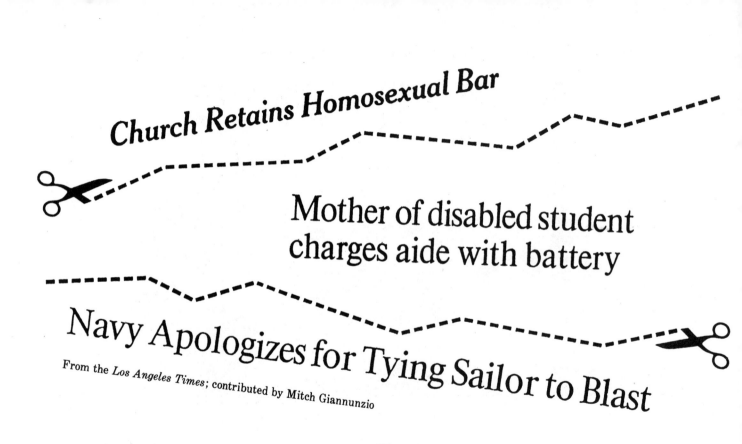

Church Retains Homosexual Bar

Mother of disabled student charges aide with battery

Navy Apologizes for Tying Sailor to Blast

From the *Los Angeles Times*; contributed by Mitch Giannunzio

**We'd tell you what it is, but that would ruin the surprise.**

Photo contributed by Allan A. Miller

# Get your sheets their whitest.

Photo contributed by Ron Coles

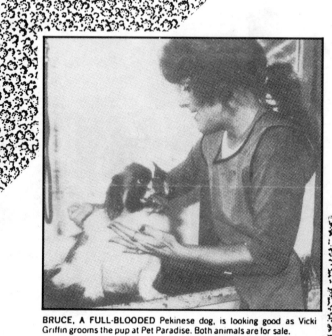

From the (Jefferson, Indiana) *Evening News*; contributed by Angela Carpenter

BRUCE, A FULL-BLOODED Pekinese dog, is looking good as Vicki Griffin grooms the pup at Pet Paradise. Both animals are for sale.

Ford

Unsuitable for motors

Photo contributed by
H. D. Meatwagon

COCKTAILS

Photo contributed by Lori Irving

# IMPORTANT
## PLEASE READ YOUR AD
for errors the first day it appears. The Press-Enterprise Co. assumes no responsibility after the first insertion.
If you are placing an ad, correcting one or canceling one, PLEASE check your ad! All claims for adjustment must be made within 15 days after expiration of ad.

Contributed by Jon Fraser

## Alone at last.

A PRIVATE WORLD - For you & your dong. See this cozy 1-2 bedroom home with its own fenced-dog run. In the 20's - and Owner wants it Sold Now!
SHERRY FRANKVILLE

Photo contributed by Phillip Kuhlenbeck

# Plates? Wow, who won the lottery?!

Ad on a building in Brooklyn, New York;
photo contributed by Thomas M. Callahan

# We're a small but proud town.

Photo contributed by John Naas

# The Amazing New
# Pull-Off Cap

From the *Chicago Tribune*;
contributed by Steve Phillips

41

# That's it, I'm getting rid of that hair ball once and for all!

From the *Arizona Daily Star*;
contributed by John M. Anderson

1163

MORTUARY
AFFAIRS
&
FOOD SERVICE
SVCS. BR., DOL, PSF

Photo contributed by Allston James

# Multiple-personality rapist sentenced to two life terms

From the Greensboro (North Carolina) *News & Record*; contributed by Lee Vernon

# Relief groups help hurt family

From the Escondido (California) *Times-Advocate*; contributed by Marianne Roberts

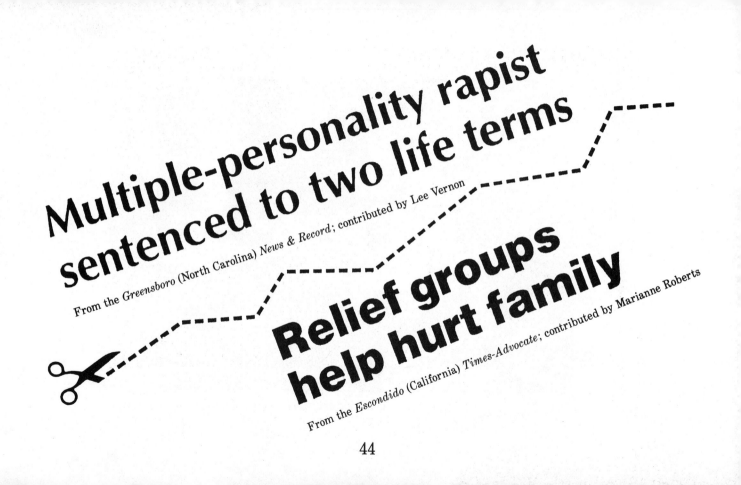

**The Thurlows,** *pictured here with their daughter Madelaine, were watching* St. Elsewhere *on television when their house in Birmingham, England, caught fire. A fireman said that Mrs. Thurlow and her two daughters continued watching the show as the house burned around them. "One of the daughters was smoking a cigarette. The wife was coughing." Firefighters removed the three women, a dog, and a "big fluffy cat" without injury.*
From the *Baltimore Evening Sun*; contributed by J. Dimeler

**Let's just say the sheriff doesn't want any trouble around here.**

Photo contributed by Pedar Ness

# Rejected boyfriend kills pets

POMPANO BEACH, Fla. (AP) — A man angry over a broken romance killed his ex-girlfriend's pet birds, stole her cat and stomped her daughter's bunny to death, police said.

Daniel R. Baxter, 35, was being held Tuersday at the Broward County Jail in lieu of $50,000 bail on charges of burglary and theft and cruelty to animals.

During the past few weeks, Kim Long reported two of her birds had been killed and two were missing. And a neighbor reported seeing Baxter take Long's cat, which has not been found, authorities said.

Baxter showed up a short time later at a Fort Lauderdale restaurant where Ms. Long works and was arrested after smashing her windshield, police said.

# Senator Slips Pork to City

■ Tarky Lombardi kept a $600,000 grant to Syracuse under wraps until the state legislative session adjourned. He was afraid Cuomo might kill the measure.

**By LUTHER F. BLIVEN**
*Albany Bureau*

A surprise $600,000 legislative grant for the city of Syracuse will be unveiled today by state Sen. Tarky Lombardi at a news conference in Syracuse.

The previously unannounced allocation was tucked away in one of the last-minute budget cleanup and supplemental spending bills passed by lawmakers in the closing hours of last week's windup meeting for the 1992 legislative session.

**File photo**

**State Sen. Tarky Lombardi got a windfall for Syracuse.**

The grant was so closely guarded that some Syracuse-area legislators won't know they voted for it until Lombardi's news conference today. The Syracuse Republican kept the appropriation secret until the legislative session was over for fear Gov. Mario Cuomo would get wind of the allocation and ax it before lawmakers left town.

The money will help ease Syracuse through a major fiscal crisis that has plagued Mayor Tom Young for months and which could have resulted in a sizable budget deficit by the end of the year.

The city's award-winning "Safe Streets" program was used as the hook on which to hang the $600,000 allocation.

"The monies would be used to continue the city's highly successful 'Safe Streets' or 'Team Oriented Policing' program, whic[h] is now operating in city neighbo[r]hoods," Lombardi said. Officers i[n] the program operate out of a tra[il]er that moves to different neig[h]borhoods to help residents solv[e] problems involving crime, housin[g] and social services.

The $600,000 grant will fre[e] up city money now used for th[e] police program to finance som[e]thing else, Lombardi said.

The senator said the $600,00[0] replaces a similar amount Youn[g] had expected to receive from a proposed horse-racing theater. The city had asked Syracuse-are[a] legislators to sponsor a bill autho[rizing a public referendum on th[e] theater. The first $416,000 o[f] betting revenues from the theater were to be earmarked for the arts.

**(See LOMBARDI, Page A-4)**

From the (Syracuse) *Post-Standard*; contributed by Casey J. Dickinson

**It's the happiest place on earth!**

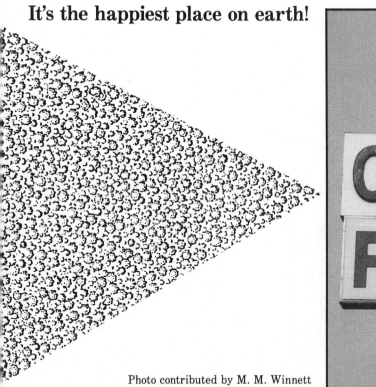

Photo contributed by M. M. Winnett

Sexual harassment
...it's everyone's
responsibility.

Ad published by the Administrative
and Clerical Officers' Association
of Sydney, Australia;
contributed by Ian James

acoa

50

FOR SALE-One Inflatable sheep. Slightly used. $15.00. Call Terry.

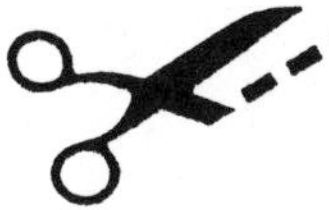

FARM SLAUGHTERING - we slaughter your animal on the farm with our truck. Galesburg Locker,

**PIER 34 IS NOT HIRING!**

- Waitresses
- Bus Persons
- Kitchen Help

Apply In person, between 10:00 a.m. and 4:00 p.m., Monday through Friday.

3011 W. Ogden Ave., Naperville

**DARKROOM TECHNIQUES**

March/April 1980
Vol. 4, No. 2

$2.95

Developing Your First
Roll of B&W Film

Super Color Dupes From
Professional Equipment

Variable Contrast Advance
Ilford Multigrade II Paper

Senator Howard Baker's
Washington Photos

From a cover for the magazine
*Darkroom Techniques*;
contributed by James P. Schwartz, Jr.

52

**Adults only, please.**

Photo contributed by Dave Law

53

Photo contributed
by R. B. Welch

54

# Hey, some of these guys don't even have cars.

Photo contributed by Casey Batule

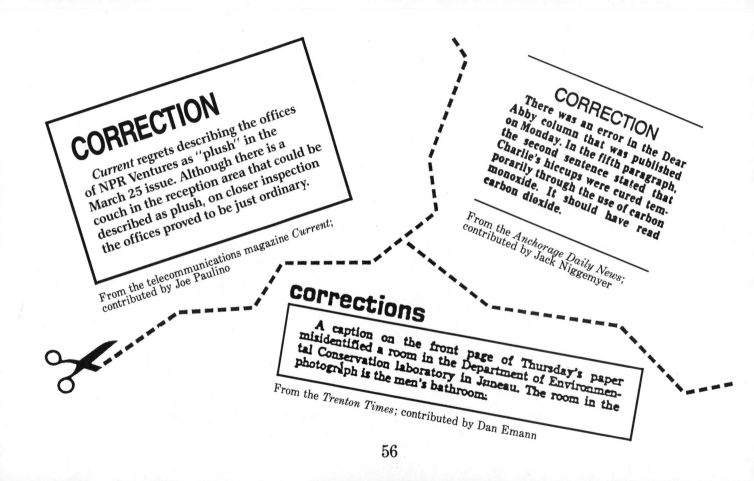

# CORRECTION

*Current* regrets describing the offices of NPR Ventures as "plush" in the March 25 issue. Although there is a couch in the reception area that could be described as plush, on closer inspection the offices proved to be just ordinary.

From the telecommunications magazine *Current*; contributed by Joe Paulino

# CORRECTION

There was an error in the Dear Abby column that was published on Monday. In the fifth paragraph, the second sentence stated that Charlie's hiccups were cured temporarily through the use of carbon monoxide. It should have read carbon dioxide.

From the *Anchorage Daily News*; contributed by Jack Niggemyer

# corrections

A caption on the front page of Thursday's paper misidentified a room in the Department of Environmental Conservation laboratory in Juneau. The room in the photograph is the men's bathroom.

From the *Trenton Times*; contributed by Dan Emann

Let's see, I have twenty minutes before I'm due back at the office,
what to do . . . what to do . . .

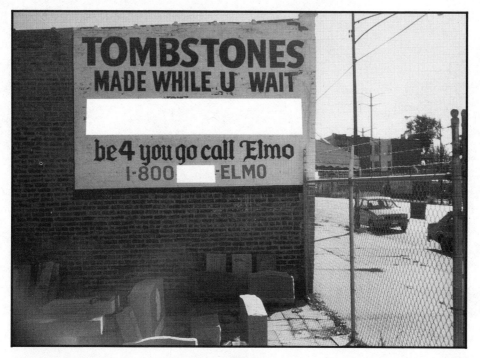

Photo contributed by Bill Edie

Photo contributed by Brian Grady

Photo contributed by M. M. Winnett

60

# Teen Jailed in Snatch

## Stripper resents exposure

## Ball a bag lady in 'Stone Pillow'

# Landlords evict Supreme Court

Can't we just refer to them as being "physically challenged"?

Photo contributed by Al Dombrowski

Photo contributed by Karen McGillivray

OK, but first I want my mechanic to look at the tomatoes.

WANTED: 1967-72 muscle car; finished, unfinished, will trade dehydrated fruits, vegetables, macaroni, tomatoes, rice, flour, lemonade, 30 year shelf life. ████ MI.

Despite the poor weather conditions, the Devils held their own against Houghton.

From the (Fredonia, New York) *Leader*; contributed by Brian Telander

Photo contributed
by Stephen P. Jones

# It takes a big man to admit when he's wrong.

## DEBBIE?

About that night I cracked up your new BMW over a concrete traffic barrier on Lake Shore Drive, I'm really sorry. What a horrible accident. When I crawled out the window you were still unconscious. I tried to pull you through, but your foot was stuck in the glove compartment. So I went to get help. I was less than fifty feet away when the gas tank exploded. Wow-Wee! Talk about explosions! I ran back and put out the fire with a wet beach blanket. THEN YOU WERE GONE! No Debbie! Where did you go? Are you okay? How's your foot? How's the car? Did they find your left arm? Look, I know you're probably a little upset. You have every right to be a little upset. I can understand that. But I don't think we should blow this thing up all out of proportion. In fact, I don't want to see anything else blow up for a long, long time. So, give me a call, or drop me a line. Let's be friends. Come over and we can play records and bang on my drums. Tell you Mom I said Hi.

Box 4499

67

Side-by-side ads from the *Honolulu Star-Bulletin*; contributed by Jerry Gauthier

68

# You know, I remember when women weren't even allowed to vote.

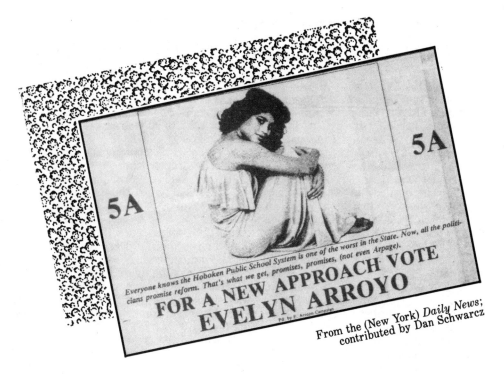

5A

5A

Everyone knows the Hoboken Public School System is one of the worst in the State. Now, all the politicians promise reform. That's what we get, promises, promises, (not even Arpage).

## FOR A NEW APPROACH VOTE
## EVELYN ARROYO

Pd by E. Arroyo Campaign

From the (New York) *Daily News*; contributed by Dan Schwarcz

**Boss is coming, quick, hide that thing!**

# Marijuana found in tuna can

**ARDSLEY, N.Y.** (AP) — The black spot in the can of tuna made Rita Shafer curious. What looked like a partially smoked marijuana cigarette on the lid made her incredulous.

"I couldn't believe it was there," Shafer said Wednesday, the day after she opened the can of Bumble Bee albacore tuna to make lunch for her 3-year-old daughter Brandi.

Bumble Bee can't quite believe it, either, and a spokeswoman said the company wants to look at the can.

"We've never had anything like this happen," said Deborah Streeter, administrator of consumer affairs for Bumble Bee. "It's very serious, if it's true. We've taken the code and we're tracking where and when it was packed." The can was sealed in California.

Bumble Bee asked her to send the can back to its headquarters in San Diego.

No recall was contemplated at this time, Streeter said.

Streeter said the company has stringent quality control standards and such an incident is unlikely. She said the tuna is still safe because the product goes through a heat sterilization process to kill germs and bacteria.

Shafer said she figured someone either put it in the can as a joke or was stealing a smoke and had to hide it because someone was coming his way.

The incident "really blew my mind," she added.

# Born leader.

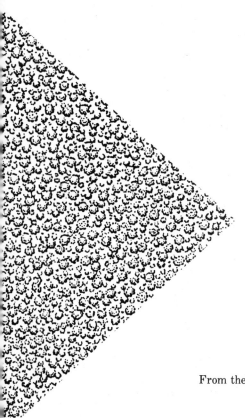

TERRY
BARRY

FOR
CITY
COUNCIL

"I'm schizophrenic
and happy."

From the *Greensboro Daily News*; contributed by Teraesa Whitley

# Screw 'em if they can't take a joke.

## Bus driver who hit dog quits job

PORT WASHINGTON, Wis. (AP) — A school bus driver insists he was joking when he shouted "Should I hit the dog?" moments before running over the animal that belonged to two of his young passengers.

The 44-year-old driver quit Thursday while the Ozaukee County district attorney considered a recommendation by the sheriff's office to file a charge of animal mistreatment. Sheriff's Lt. Keith Gross said investigators concluded the man ran over the dog intentionally Jan. 26.

Among nine students on the bus were two children whose family owned the dog, a 17-month-old Brittany spaniel named Chelsea.

Melissa Monahan, mother of the 9-year-old girl and 11-year-old boy said the dog often came up to the road when it saw the bus.

From the *Cedar Rapids Daily Tribune*;
contributed by Dale Bowden

Photo contributed by Peter Lorenz

Photo contributed by Chuck Prosek

From the (Medford, Oregon) *Mail Tribune*; contributed by R. J. Holmes

The Folger Consort will be hard at 10 a.m. Christmas Day.

# City to control beaver with contraceptive

Associated Press

WHEAT RIDGE — A female beaver, too young to breed and establish her own lodge on Clear Creek, has lost her reproductive chance after being fitted with a Norplant contraceptive device.

Littleton veterinarian David Robinson performed the implant Thursday — the first such sterilization of a beaver in the state.

The city of Wheat Ridge, eager to find a humane method of controlling beaver populations, teamed up with Wildlife 2000, an environmental group working with the Colorado Division of Wildlife to experiment with beaver contraception.

"It just took a few minutes and was far less painful than if she had been given a tubal ligation, which we have done to sterilize beaver in the past," Wildlife 2000 president Sherri Tippie said.

# *Heil* Al Greenwood.

**Honey, look what I found hidden under Junior's mattress.**

Photo contributed by Darrell Garrison

Photo contributed by Elizabeth Sims

Photo contributed by Michael Ritto

# Family fun.

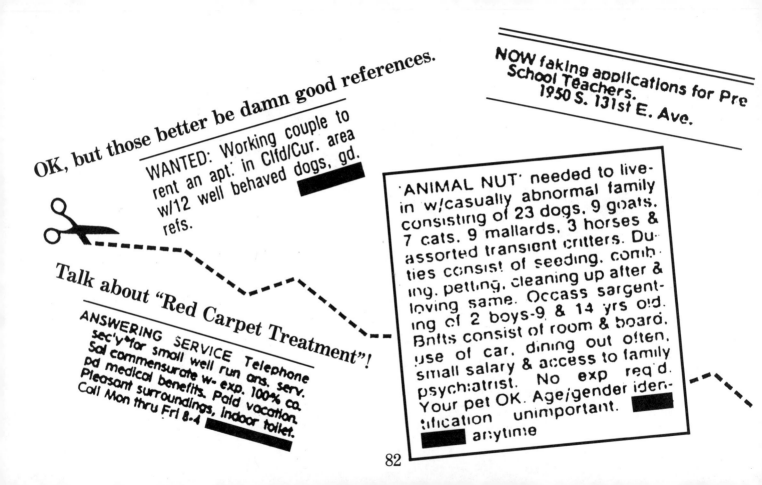

*OK, but those better be damn good references.*

WANTED: Working couple to rent an apt. in Clfd/Cur. area w/12 well behaved dogs, gd. refs. ███

NOW faking applications for Pre School Teachers. 1950 S. 131st E. Ave.

*Talk about "Red Carpet Treatment"!*

ANSWERING SERVICE Telephone sec'y for small well run ans. serv. Sal commensurate w- exp. 100% co. pd medical benefits. Paid vacation. Pleasant surroundings. Indoor toilet. Call Mon thru Fri 8-4 ███

'ANIMAL NUT' needed to live-in w/casually abnormal family consisting of 23 dogs, 9 goats, 7 cats, 9 mallards, 3 horses & assorted transient critters. Duties consist of seeding, combing, petting, cleaning up after & loving same. Occass sargenting of 2 boys-9 & 14 yrs old. Bnfts consist of room & board, use of car, dining out often, small salary & access to family psychiatrist. No exp req'd. Your pet OK. Age/gender identification unimportant. ███ anytime

82

**In fact, just stay away from my daughter altogether!**

Photo contributed by Paul Smith

From the *San Diego Tribune*; contributed by Tony Slad

# Who says the Swiss never contribute anything to mankind?

● A SWISS inventor tests his hinged bicycle in Zurich. The inventor, who sensibly prefers that his name not be used, said the idea seemed to make sense when he thought of it. But, after riding it, he admits it makes no sense. He added: "We live in a world where every little thing is supposed to make sense, and I'm tired of that."

Photo contributed by Sherrie Roden

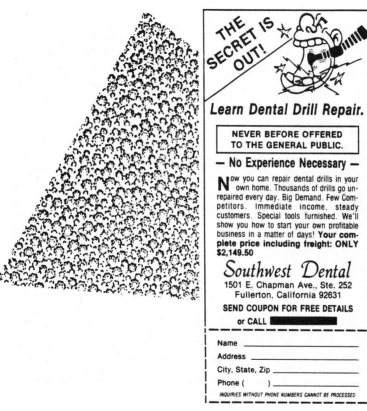

Members of Gay Men's Chorus of Los Angeles, who usually wear tuxedos for concerts, don expressive costumes for "Hidden Legacies" performances.

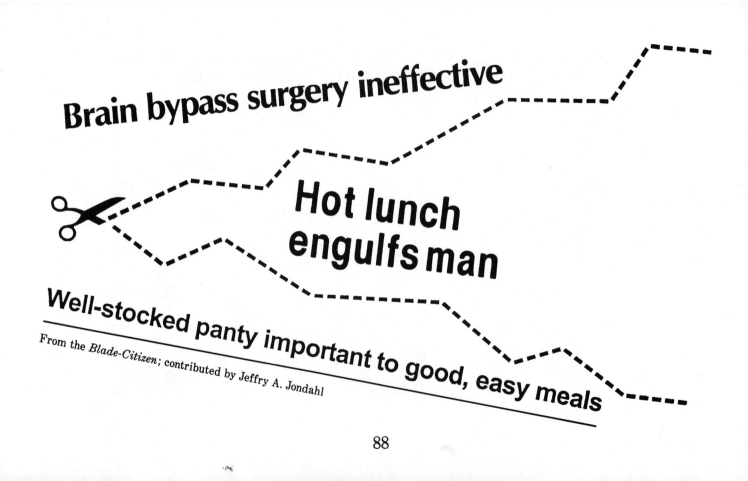

Brain bypass surgery ineffective

Hot lunch
engulfs man

Well-stocked panty important to good, easy meals

From the *Blade-Citizen*; contributed by Jeffry A. Jondahl

Photo contributed by M. M. Winnett

# CORRECTION

In the story Saturday about animal control work in Paso Robles, the featured quotation was incorrectly attributed to Robert Dollahite, director of the county Animal Regulation Department.

That statement, "I drive to work everyday watching dead cats getting flatter and flatter" was actually made by Richard Deming, Paso Robles city manager.

*From the San Luis Obispo County Telegram-Tribune; contributed by Toni Spencer*

# CORRECTION

Due to an error in transcription, Danielle Brisebois was misrepresented in US ("Where Are They Now?" US 60). Discussing the demands of the acting profession, Brisebois was misquoted as saying, "You have to know how to run, you have to be in shape, you have to know how to do sex acts." She actually said, "You have to know how to do circus acts." *US* regrets the error.

*From US magazine; contributed by David Masella*

# Correction

A story about parolee Newt Becknell in Sunday's *Enquirer* incorrectly said that he was married. By an editing error, Becknell was described as single.

# Corrections

A story in Sunday editions stated that parolee Newt Becknell is married. He is single. A correction Monday failed to make that clear.

*From two consecutive issues of the Cincinnati Enquirer; contributed by Rosanna Hoberg*

90

**Uh oh, Spot's chasing those invisible cats from Venus again.**

Photo contributed by Jim Auiles

**I guess everyone has their own interpretation of the Bible.**

Photo contributed by Wendy Cowden

Photo contributed by T. A. McDermid

# Stop laughing, you insensitive bastards!

**IN MEMORIAM**

In memory of Steve "Mike" Detmer who was killed by a bowling ball on January 4, 1985.

We will never forget you.

June Detmer,
Ann Detmer &
Ernie Detmer

## 100% ACRYLIC
# WARM-UP SUIT

- Top quality warm-up suit
- Great for today's jogger
- Machine washable
- Full-length zipper on jacket

Similar to Illustration

REG 19.99

**15.44** SET

Part of an ad from the *Kansas City Star*;
contributed by James Mercer

96

Photo contributed by Susan E. Henry

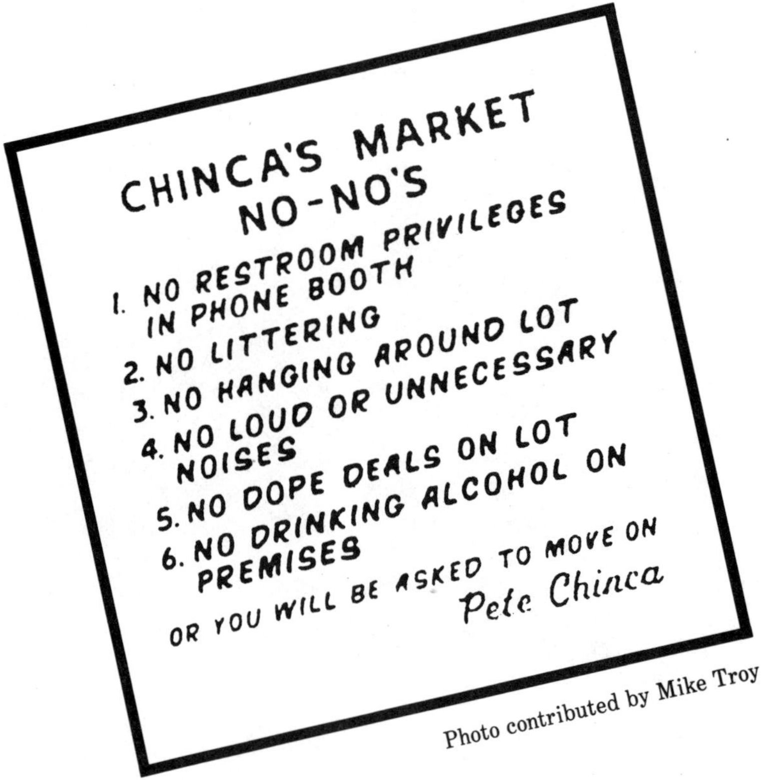

CHINCA'S MARKET
NO-NO'S

1. NO RESTROOM PRIVILEGES IN PHONE BOOTH
2. NO LITTERING
3. NO HANGING AROUND LOT
4. NO LOUD OR UNNECESSARY NOISES
5. NO DOPE DEALS ON LOT
6. NO DRINKING ALCOHOL ON PREMISES

OR YOU WILL BE ASKED TO MOVE ON

Pete Chinca

Photo contributed by Mike Troy

98

Photo contributed by Brian Galford

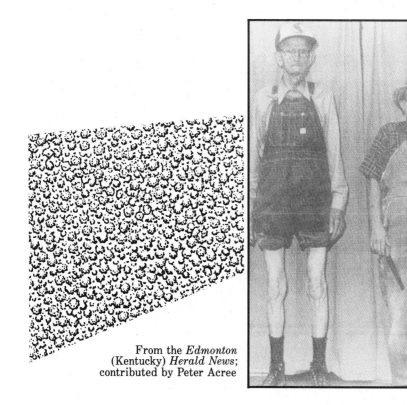

From the *Edmonton*
(Kentucky) *Herald News*;
contributed by Peter Acree

**Albert Francis was the knobby
knee winner and Alma Parrigan
won the hog calling contest.**

**7 5 20 Legmen** Jack falls for a college student who is also a part-time hooker in trouble with a white-slavery ring operator intent on killing her. 1 hr.

**23 MOVIE** ★½ "Helter Skelter" (1949, Comedy) Carol Marsh, David Tomlinson. A detective gets involved with a wealthy socialite who can't seem to stop hiccupping. (2 hrs.)

**9.10 Superman** (Rpt) (G)
**9.30 Woody Woodpecker:** 21 Billion Dollar Boner (Rpt) (G)

**Dick Van Dyke** Rob, under the influence of science fiction, fears that a walnut will steal his imagination and his thumbs.

# Get it in writing.

"My husband and I have an understanding: He won't track dirt in my house while he's living and I won't pack 6 feet of it in his face when he's dead. I'm going to **Locust Hill Chapel Mausoleum** and get a pair of crypts while they're available and the price is low!"

Why don't you call ███████ also.

Photo contributed by Laurence Faith

# You live on the corner of *where*?

Photo contributed by Thomas Lines

From the *Sacramento* (California) *Bee*; contributed by Joe Milton

# Stop . . . you're *both* right.

Photo contributed by Dale Schultz

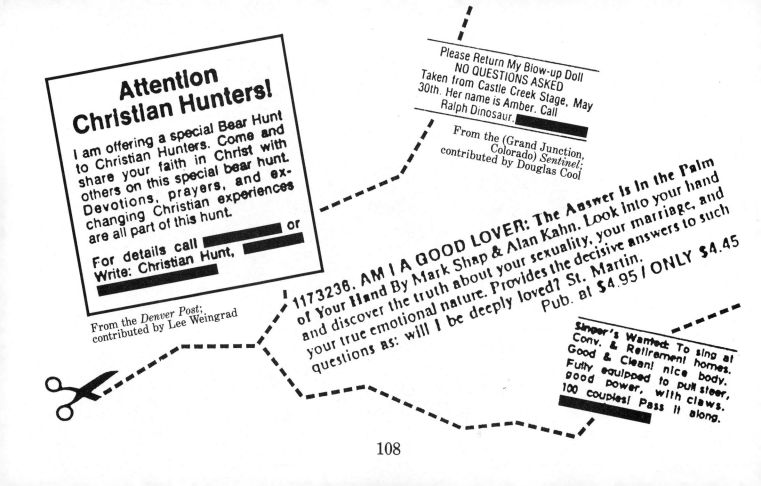

## Attention Christian Hunters!

I am offering a special Bear Hunt to Christian Hunters. Come and share your faith in Christ with others on this special bear hunt. Devotions, prayers, and ex-changing Christian experiences are all part of this hunt.

For details call ▮▮▮▮▮ or Write: Christian Hunt, ▮▮▮▮▮

From the *Denver Post*;
contributed by Lee Weingrad

Please Return My Blow-up Doll
NO QUESTIONS ASKED
Taken from Castle Creek Stage, May 30th. Her name is Amber. Call Ralph Dinosaur, ▮▮▮▮▮

From the (Grand Junction, Colorado) *Sentinel*; contributed by Douglas Cool

1173238. AM I A GOOD LOVER: The Answer Is In the Palm of Your Hand By Mark Shap & Alan Kahn. Look into your hand and discover the truth about your sexuality, your marriage, and your true emotional nature. Provides the decisive answers to such questions as: will I be deeply loved? St. Martin. Pub. at $4.95 / ONLY $4.45

Singer's Wanted: To sing at Conv. & Retirement homes. Good & Clean! nice body. Fully equipped to pull steer, good power, with claws. 100 couples! Pass it along.

From an International
House of Pancakes place mat;
contributed by Joe Traynor

Items that are round and wrinkled stand out among nutritious foods

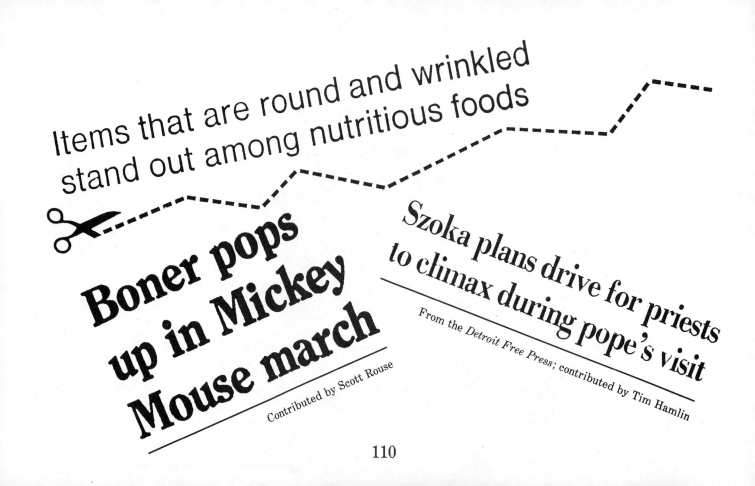

# Boner pops up in Mickey Mouse march

Contributed by Scott Rouse

# Szoka plans drive for priests to climax during pope's visit

From the *Detroit Free Press*; contributed by Tim Hamlin

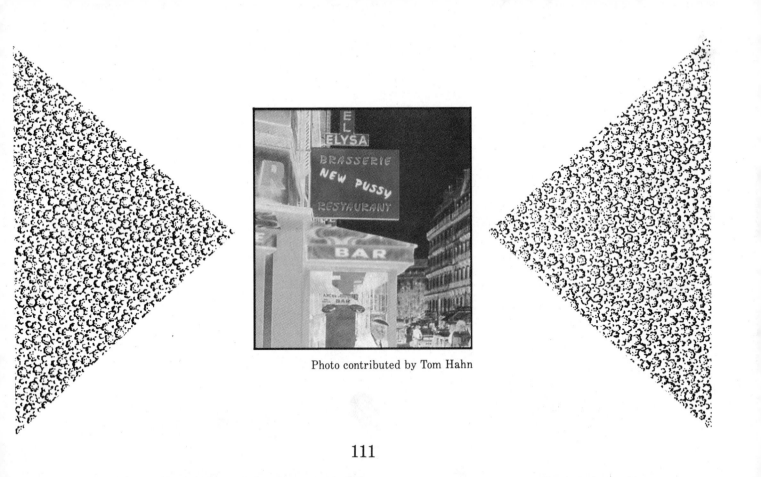

Photo contributed by Tom Hahn

111

**Whoa, slow down, doc,
so those of us without a medical degree can keep up with you.**

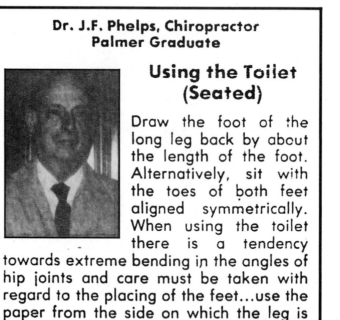

**Dr. J.F. Phelps, Chiropractor
Palmer Graduate**

## Using the Toilet (Seated)

Draw the foot of the long leg back by about the length of the foot. Alternatively, sit with the toes of both feet aligned symmetrically. When using the toilet there is a tendency towards extreme bending in the angles of hip joints and care must be taken with regard to the placing of the feet...use the paper from the side on which the leg is long.

From the *Gwinnet* (Michigan) *Daily News*; contributed by Mark R. Coulston

Photo contributed by Judy Lalley

113

Photo contributed by Bruce Markoe

# One-stop shopping.

Photo contributed by Patrick Hammer

115

# Quick, who's got a quarter?

Photo contributed by Michael Viapiana

# You've got one *sick* family, pal.

Photo contributed
by R. J. Swanson

Photo contributed
by Frank Brennan

# Thank God, now I can finally get rid of the embarassing name "Cockman."

**Dr. and Mrs. Donald Dickman**

## Cockman-Dickman

Carrie Anne Cockman, formerly of Davenport, and Dr. Donald G. Dickman, Cheyenne, Wyo., were married May 29 at St. John's Church, Creighton University, Omaha, Neb.

Their attendants were Maureen Maley, Maureen Mullin, Julie Stockert, Peggy Dickman, Pam Dickman, Kari Greguska, Troy Peterson, John Sammis, Ben Lass, Chris Cockman and Joe Cockman.

Their parents are Len and Lory Cockman, Newton, Iowa; and Charles and Shirley Dickman, Cheyenne.

# Can you make me look like Keith Richards?

Photo contributed by Doug Smith

Photo contributed by John Purcell

**Those fitness geeks will eat anything.**

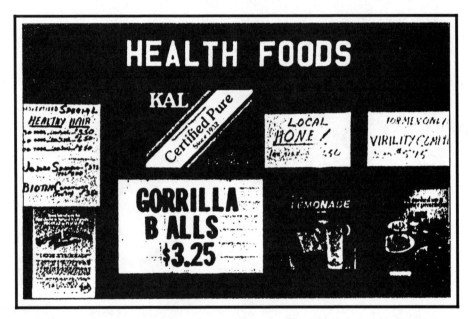

Photo contributed by Bill Whiting

**50 Movie: "Lady Liberty"** Sophia Loren. An Italian woman on her way to a wedding-attempts to go through customs with a large sausage (1972) ★★

**12 Star Trek** Mr. Spoc) blows his cool and almost gets Capt. Kirk killed when an overwhelming mating urge takes possession of him. (To 3:30)

12:00 **2 Vega$** Dan frantically searches for a large quantity of cocaine. (R)

## We were getting some complaints.

Photo contributed by Julia T. Momenko

# I swear, that man doesn't look a day over 75.

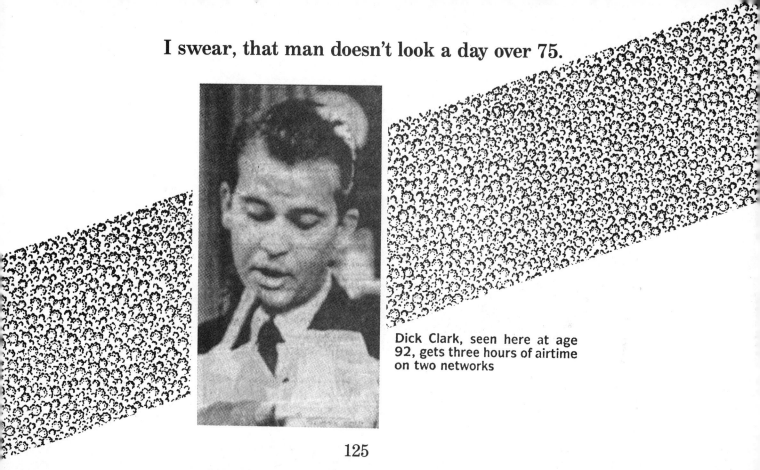

Dick Clark, seen here at age 92, gets three hours of airtime on two networks

Photo contributed by Michael Kiriazis

**Put on your prettiest evening gown, dear, we're going dancing!**

Photo contributed by Pedar Ness

# If Astros win, will they come?

**BY GENE DUFFEY**
OF THE HOUSTON POST STAFF

The earth moved Sunday morning in California and still the fans made it to Dodger Stadium, 26,260 ignoring the earthquake and paying to see Los Angeles

*From the Houston Post*

# Officials warn clams, oysters can carry virus

# Shortage of Brains Slows Medical Research

# Why, Jane, your cervical collar, it's . . . it's . . . gorgeous!

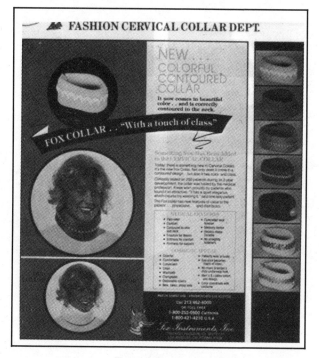

From a Fox Instruments, Inc., catalog

THE GIRL COMES FIRST IN GIRL SCOUTING

Contributed by Nancy Rimassa

130

# Whatever happened to $2.00 a minute?

BUILDINGS - "ONE PHONE CALL CAN GIVE YOU a low cost erection." by direct telephone order from Ontario Manufacturer...28 x30 Value $3,700. Now $2,944. 40x50 Value $6,800. Now $5,593. Other sizes available 1-800-████████ Pioneer first in Steel Buildings since 1980.

From the (Canada) *News Advertiser*; contributed by Martin Roncetti

# Sex Ed. 101.

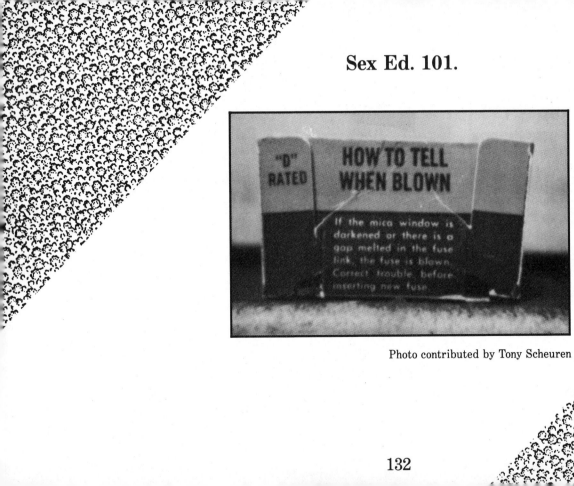

Photo contributed by Tony Scheuren

# A doctor who truly empathizes with his patients.

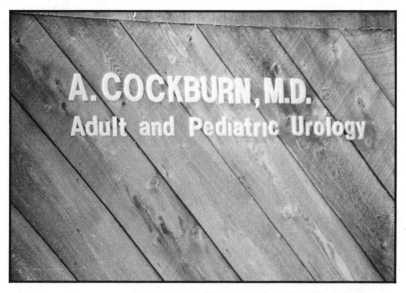

Photo contributed by Mark A. Barroso

Photo contributed by Jeffrey Cohen

Coupon contributed by B. Hertz

**Boy, it sure pays to advertise!**

Photo contributed by Peter Brown

Photo contributed by Ted Goldsmith

Why don't you stay home tonight, honey—
I don't mind going to the garage by myself.

"FREE" *

We Do Head Jobs!

Aluminum head welding          Pressure testing
Camline repair and boring      Surfacing
Camshaft grinding and repair   Rocker arm grinding
       *free deck warpage check
       *free valve leakage check ($15.00 value)

SUPERIOR
HEAD 5 SERVICE    1-800-■■■■■■
                  FREYA and BROADWAY

From *Wheel Deals*; contributed by Boob Jackson

# Small-town entertainment.

# See you next year, babe.

**A family affair.** A good time was had by all who attended the Celebrity Rodeo and Longhorn Cattle Drive.

Photo contributed by Anne Pellegrino

# Oh no, it's Tony Danza!

Photo contributed by Pedar Ness

**⑧ ⑫ Just Kidding** Topics children discuss include why cows don't wear pants, and what to do with a shotgun at the dinner table. (Repeat)

✂ ----

**㉔ CBN 700 Club** Abortion facts; the NFL's greatest bloopers.

(CMX) **Movie** ★ ''The Beast Within'' (1982) Ronny Cox, Bibi Besch. A woman is raped on her honeymoon by a hairy-legged creature. 'R'

**❼ MOVIE** ★TENTACLES (Thriller, 1977). What has eight legs, no nose an eats people? Shelley Winters. (1 hr. 50 min.)

143

# Who says we're not open-minded?

Photo contributed by L. Moskow

Quick, Larry, it's my only chance!——

# Man beats off bear to save his friend

# Democrats welcome Dicks this year at party's 'big love-in'

Photo contributed by Clark Risley

**The power of persuasion.**

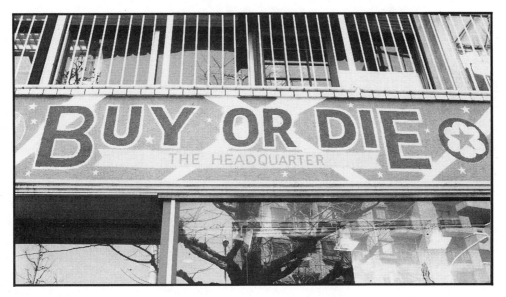

Photo contributed by Gary Curtis

Almost as prestigious as the John Holmes Cup.

# Record-setting Wang wins Jesse Owens Trophy

From the *Duluth News-Tribune*; contributed by Jack Fiamoncini

My God, someone get this poor victim some counseling!

# Holdup for pleasure

Canadian Press

MONTREAL — A man held a gun on a taxi driver while his female companion performed oral sex on the cabbie, police said.

Provincial police said the cab driver told them the woman later tipped him $24.

The 40-year-old cabbie, identified only as Michel, picked up a couple early Sunday in Chambly, south of Montreal.

He said the woman, in her 20s, who was sitting beside him on the front seat, propositioned him as he was driving, police said.

When he refused her advances, her male companion, who was in his 50s, pressed the barrel of a handgun to his head and ordered him to let the woman have her way.

The cabbie said he kept driving as the woman performed oral sex.

He was later ordered to drive to suburban Longueuil, where the couple got out.

The cabbie told police the woman paid the $26 fare with a $50 bill and told him to keep the change.

From the Canadian newspaper *The Province*; contributed by Kevin Vancancius

Hmm, that's the fourth guy today asking for Cissy.

**Grandma's age-old recipe.**

Photo contributed by Gail Heim

Photo contributed by Pedar Ness

Photo contributed by James Lola

Photo contributed by Ray Check

## Street - Lay

Mr. and Mrs. Dean Street of Toledo are pleased to announce the engagement of their daughter, Diane Lynn, to Lonnie T. Lay, son of Mr. and Mrs. Arzo Lay of Toledo.

A March 27, 1993 wedding is planned.

# Thompson's pen is a sword

## Peters to pull out of two city projects

By Jeff B. Hansen
News staff writer

company be allowed to discontinue work on two city projects.

In a separate prepared statement

fraud charges by city attorneys and the state Attorney General's Office.

unfair and biased articles ...

From the *Birmingham* (Alabama) *News*; contributed by Steve Elliot

## The joy of pubic worship

From the *St. Charles* (Missouri) *Journal*; contributed by Bob Swain

## Love-Organ

SHERWOOD — Mary Theresa Organ and Robert Sterling Love were married Saturday in Immaculate Conception Catholic Church by the Rev. John O'Donnell. Parents are Mr. and Mrs. Thomas P. Organ and Mr. and Mrs. Robert E. Love, all of Sherwood.

Honor attendants were Lori Howard and Victor Cummings. The couple will reside in North Little Rock.

*From the Arkansas Gazette;*
*contributed by Jack Finch*

MRS. ROBERT LOVE

Hey Dad, when you pick
me up at school tomorrow,
can you take the Volvo instead?

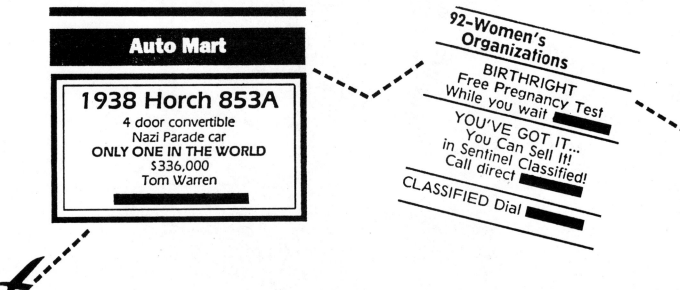

**Auto Mart**

# 1938 Horch 853A
4 door convertible
Nazi Parade car
**ONLY ONE IN THE WORLD**
$336,000
Tom Warren

**92–Women's Organizations**

BIRTHRIGHT
Free Pregnancy Test
While you wait

YOU'VE GOT IT...
You Can Sell It!
in Sentinel Classified!
Call direct

CLASSIFIED Dial

Photo contributed by Thomas Powell

## Swallows, Wright

Kim Raquel Swallows and Robert Craig Wright exchanged wedding vows in a 2 p.m. ceremony on July 30 at the Eastside Kirtland Air Force Base Chapel.

The bride is the daughter of Kathleen M. Swallows of Honolulu. The groom's parents are Mr. and Mrs. Keith Wright of Northville, Mich.

Gina Swallows and Deidre Montaño, sisters of the bride, were attendants.

**Mrs. Wright**

Keith Wright, the groom's father, was best man.

The couple spent their honeymoon in Telluride, Colo. and Durango, Colo.

They are making their home in Rio Rancho, where the bride is a homemaker and the groom is a technical sergeant of Life Support serving in the United States Air Force.

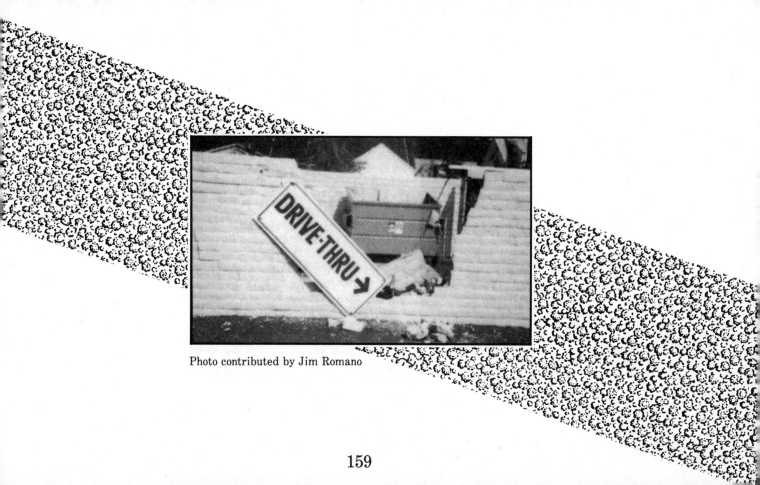

Photo contributed by Jim Romano

Photo contributed by Steve Jones

Photo contributed by Steve Jones

Photo contributed by Joe Bissin

Photo contributed by Susan Hoffman

**It sounds so beautiful when you put it that way.**

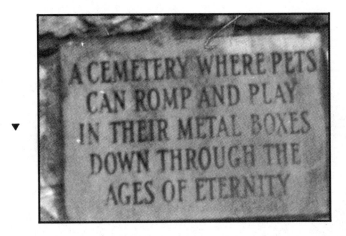

A CEMETERY WHERE PETS
CAN ROMP AND PLAY
IN THEIR METAL BOXES
DOWN THROUGH THE
AGES OF ETERNITY

Crummy
Funeral Homes

Photo contributed by John Smallwood

Photo contributed by Robert J. Wiersewa II

# Feminist leader marketing head

# Woman benefits from cancer

## Clerk reports:
# Marriages are on the rise; clamming permits down

**Hey honey, look what I found when I was cleaning out the closet.**

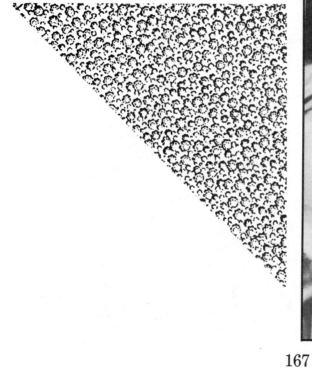

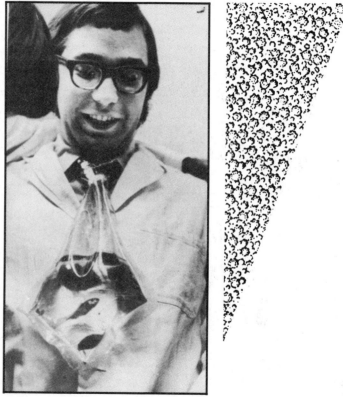

Photo contributed by Don Williams

Photo contributed by Gail Williams

Photo contributed by Alan Rose

Front and back of a pack of matches; contributed by Rodd Zolkos

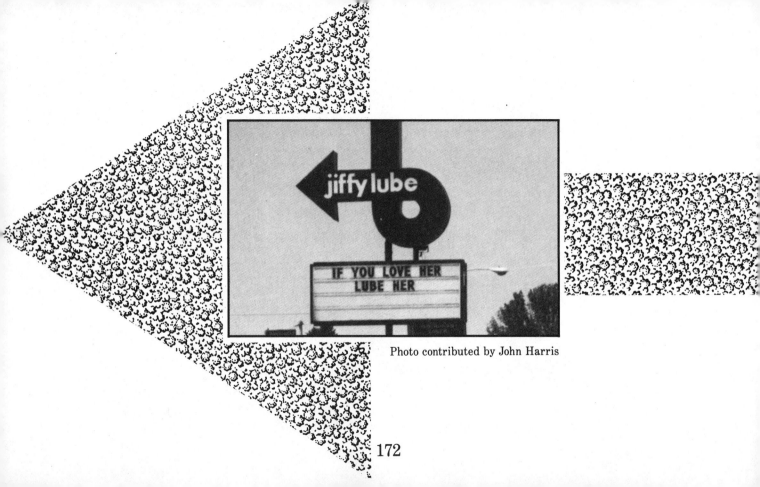

IF YOU LOVE HER
LUBE HER

Photo contributed by John Harris

172

THE SEA
HAS MOVED 1 BLOCK SOUTH
TO 305 N. HARBOR BLVD

Photo contributed by
Thomas A. Ward

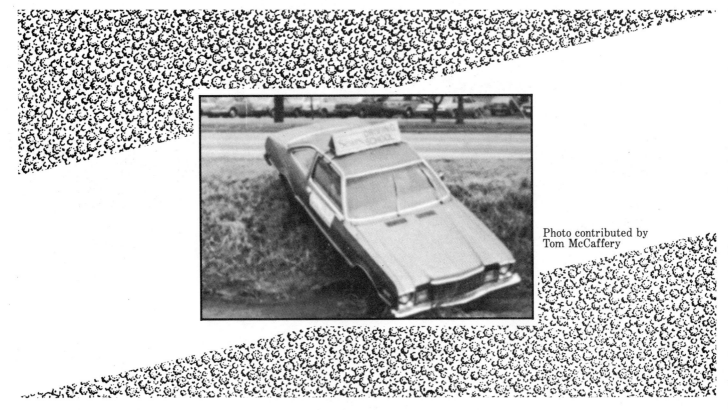

Photo contributed by
Tom McCaffery

# Disciples of Christ Name Interim Leader

From the *Los Angeles Times*; contributed by Mitch Giannunzio

# Hookers plying the Liffey thrill the crowds

From the *Irish Press*; contributed by F. Corbin

# Barter trade: Negros cocks for marijuana

From a Philippine newspaper; contributed by Lewis Brown

Please do not tap or hit    ass

Photo contributed by Teri Plotnick

176

Photo contributed by Donald R. Shreier

# When you're tired of life . . .

Photo contributed by Michael Grissom

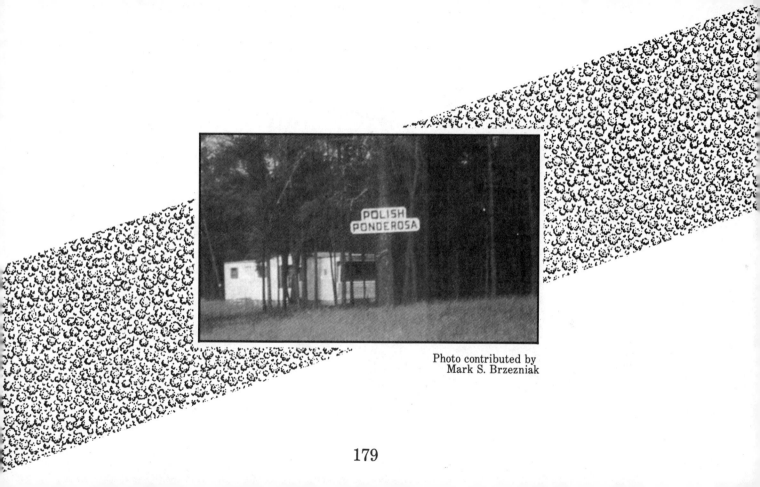

Photo contributed by
Mark S. Brzezniak

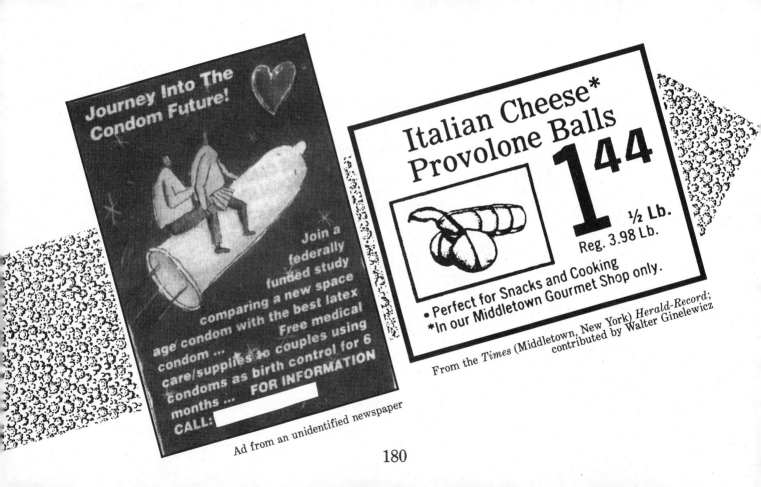

Journey Into The Condom Future!

Join a federally funded study comparing a new space age condom with the best latex condom ... Free medical care/supplies to couples using condoms as birth control for 6 months ... FOR INFORMATION CALL:

Ad from an unidentified newspaper

Italian Cheese* Provolone Balls

1 44 ½ Lb.

Reg. 3.98 Lb.

• Perfect for Snacks and Cooking
*In our Middletown Gourmet Shop only.

From the *Times* (Middletown, New York) *Herald-Record*; contributed by Walter Ginelewicz

180

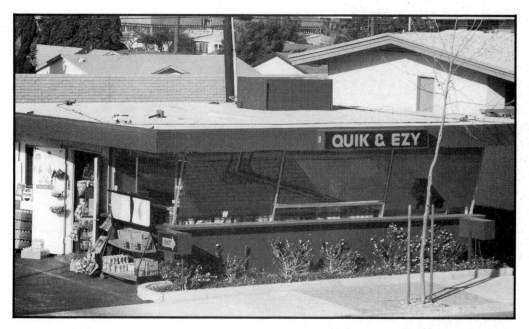

Photo contributed by Deb Jonaitis

**Lebanon will try bombing suspects**

**Coke Head To Speak Here**

*Humane society steps up pet destruction*